Applying the Standards:
Math
Grade 4

Credits
Content Editor: Amy Gamble
Copy Editor: Elise Craver, Angela Triplett

Visit *carsondellosa.com* for correlations to Common Core, state, national, and Canadian provincial standards.

Carson-Dellosa Publishing, LLC
PO Box 35665
Greensboro, NC 27425 USA
carsondellosa.com

ISBN 978-1-4838-1570-1
01-005151151

Table of Contents

Introduction

The purpose of this book is to engage students in applying the standards to real-world, higher-level thinking problems. Each Common Core mathematics standard is covered by one or more practice pages.

Students will be expected to answer a few straightforward problems to prove basic understanding of the standard. Then, they are presented with a higher-level thinking problem. These problems are designed to require students to demonstrate their complete understanding and flexibility with the standard. Finally, a reflection question guides students to review their work on the previous problem. The reflection questions are designed to support the Standards for Mathematical Practice as students are asked to study their approaches, their successes, and their struggles.

Use the included rubric to guide assessment of student responses and further plan any necessary remediation. Understanding and applying mathematical knowledge to realistic problems is an invaluable skill that will help students succeed in their school years and beyond.

Common Core Alignment Chart

Use this chart to plan your instruction, practice, or remediation of a specific standard. To do this, first choose your targeted standard; then, find the pages listed on the chart that correlate to the standard.

Common Core State Standards*		Practice Pages
Operations and Algebraic Thinking		
Use four operations with whole numbers to solve problems.	4.OA.1–4.OA.3	5–7
Gain familiarity with factors and multiples.	4.OA.4	8–10
Generate and analyze patterns.	4.OA.5	11, 12
Number and Operations in Base Ten		
Generalize place value understanding for multi-digit whole numbers.	4.NBT.1–4.NBT.3	13–16
Use place value understanding and properties of operations to perform multi-digit arithmetic.	4.NBT.4– 4.NBT.6	17–25
Number and Operations—Fractions		
Extend understanding of fraction equivalence and ordering.	4.NF.1–4.NF.2	26–29
Build fractions from unit fractions by applying and extending previous understandings of operations on whole numbers.	4.NF.3–4.NF.4	30–40
Understand decimal notation for fractions, and compare decimal fractions.	4.NF.5–4.NF.7	41–43
Measurement and Data		
Solve problems involving measurement and conversion of measurements from a larger unit to a smaller unit.	4.MD.1–4.MD.3	44–50, 62
Represent and interpret data.	4.MD.4	51
Geometric measurement: understand concepts of angle and measure angles.	4.MD.5–4.MD.7	52–56
Geometry		
Draw and identify lines and angles, and classify shapes and properties of their lines and angles.	4.G.1–4.G.3	57–62

Problem-Solving Rubric

Use this rubric as a guide to assess students' written work. It can also be offered to students to help them check their work or as a tool to show your scoring.

4
- _____ Answers all of the problems correctly
- _____ Identifies all of the key numbers and operations in the problem
- _____ Uses an appropriate and complete strategy for solving the problem
- _____ Skillfully justifies answer and strategy used
- _____ Offers insightful reasoning and strong evidence of critical thinking
- _____ Provides easy-to-understand, clear, and concise answers

3
- _____ Answers most of the problems correctly
- _____ Identifies most of the key numbers and operations in the problem
- _____ Uses an appropriate but incomplete strategy for solving the problem
- _____ Justifies answer and strategy used
- _____ Offers sufficient reasoning and evidence of critical thinking
- _____ Provides easy-to-understand answers

2
- _____ Answers some of the problems correctly
- _____ Identifies some of the key numbers and operations in the problem
- _____ Uses an inappropriate or unclear strategy for solving the problem
- _____ Attempts to justify answer and strategy used
- _____ Demonstrates some evidence of critical thinking
- _____ Provides answers that are understandable but lack focus

1
- _____ Answers most or all of the problems incorrectly
- _____ Identifies few or none of the key numbers and operations in the problem
- _____ Uses no strategy or plan for solving the problem
- _____ Does not justify answer and strategy used
- _____ Demonstrates limited or no evidence of critical thinking
- _____ Provides answers that are difficult to understand

Name _____

Rewrite each statement as a multiplication sentence.

1. three times larger than six

   _____

2. an eight-pound baby will quickly double in size

   _____

3. four times as many as nine

   _____

Solve. Show your mathematical thinking.

4. Grace collects unique buttons. Her grandmother gave her 3 buttons to start her collection. She quickly found enough buttons to triple her collection. Then, over the next year, her collection grew 8 times larger. If her collection continues to double each year after that, how many years will it be until she has over 300 buttons in her collection?

✺ Reflect

Explain a different way to solve problem 4.

_____

_____

_____

_____

_____

Name _____

Solve.

1. Andre has 6 toy robots. Davis has 7 times as many toy robots as Andre. How many toy robots does Davis have?

_____

2. Jan's savings account now has $64 in it. That is 8 times the amount she started with when she opened her account. How much money did Jan deposit when she first opened her account?

_____

Solve. Show your mathematical thinking.

3. Scientists are tracking tree growth in a young forest. An oak tree measured 9 feet tall. A nearby maple tree measured 7 feet tall. When they measured the trees again 2 years later, the oak tree was 54 feet tall, and the maple tree was 49 feet tall. Which tree grew the fastest?

Reflect

Anna claims the oak tree grew faster because it is taller than the maple tree. Is her reasoning correct? Explain.

_____

_____

_____

_____

_____

Name _____

Solve.

1. Kami has 28 shaped erasers. She gives 13 of them to her sister and shares the rest evenly between herself and 2 friends. How many erasers does Kami keep?

   _____

2. Derek scored twice as many goals in the final championship game as he had scored in the last 3 games of the season. If Derek scored 3 goals in each of the last 3 games of the season, how many goals did he score in the championship game?

   _____

Solve. Show your mathematical thinking.

3. A convention hall charges $45 per 6-person table and $57 per 8-person table for an event. If 329 people are expected to attend the event, what is the most cost-efficient combination of tables?

☀ Reflect

Explain how you can use rounding to guess which table size is the least expensive for the number of attendees.

_____

_____

_____

_____

_____

Name _____

List all of the factor pairs for each number.

1. 18

_____

2. 55

_____

3. 36

_____

4. 63

_____

Solve. Show your mathematical thinking.

5. A carpenter is building a rectangular frame from a board that is 23 feet long. He wants to make a frame with sides that are whole numbers and the largest area possible. He wants to waste the least amount of wood. What will the dimensions of the frame be?

☀ Reflect

Is it possible to make the frame without wasting any of the wood? Explain.

_____

_____

_____

Name _____

List all multiples up to 100 for each number.

1. 4

_____

2. 5

_____

3. 11

_____

4. 9

_____

Solve. Show your mathematical thinking.

5. Miranda has a large collection of thimbles. She wants to display them in groups of 3 or 6. If she has 81 thimbles, how could her collection be arranged?

☀ Reflect

Explain why knowledge of the multiples of 9 can help solve problem 5.

_____

_____

_____

Name _____

Tell whether each number is prime or composite.

1. 12

_____

2. 7

_____

3. 26

_____

4. 51

_____

Solve. Show your mathematical thinking.

5. Henry says that all even numbers are composite and all odd numbers are prime.
   Prove him right or wrong.

Reflect

How could you figure out if an odd number is prime or composite?

_____

_____

_____

_____

_____

Name _____

Write the next three numbers in each pattern.

1. 4, 9, 14, 19, _____ , _____ , _____

2. 3, 12, 48, 192, _____ , _____ , _____

3. 11, 18, 15, 22, 19, _____ , _____ , _____

4. 2, 6, 8, 24, 26, _____ , _____ , _____

Solve. Show your mathematical thinking.

5. The distances in miles to the next four highway exits are shown on a sign. A rest stop is three exits past Fawn Lane. If the pattern continues, how far away is the rest stop?

Deer Road	2 1/2
Buck Street	5 1/2
Doe Avenue	8
Fawn Lane	11

 **Reflect**

Describe the pattern of distances with fractions and without fractions.

_____

_____

_____

_____

Name _____

Draw the next image for each pattern.

1. △ ▢ △ ▢ △ ▢ △ _____

2. ▢   ▢▢   ▢▢ _____

3. ⊠ ⊠ ⊠ _____

Solve. Show your mathematical thinking.

4. A mason is creating a square patio with two types of square stones: dark gray for the border and light gray for the center. The smallest patio he can make has 8 dark gray border stones and 1 light gray stone in the center. The next size patio has 4 light gray stones in the center and 12 dark gray border stones. The client wants a patio that is 5 stones by 5 stones in the center. How many dark gray stones will the mason need for the border?

Reflect

Write a rule for how the number of dark gray border stones change. Write a rule for how the number of light gray center stones change. Explain how the two rules are different.

_____

_____

_____

_____

_____

_____

Name _____

Solve.

1. 4 hundreds = _____ tens

2. 7 tens = _____ ones

3. 20 tens = _____ hundreds

4. 5 ten thousands = _____ hundreds

Solve. Show your mathematical thinking.

5. Mr. Edwards needs to buy shaped erasers as prizes for the school fair. He found one store selling the erasers at $2 for 10 erasers. He found another store selling the erasers in bulk at $50 for 1,000 erasers. If he needs 1,000 erasers, which option is a better deal? Why?

✹ Reflect

If Mr. Edwards needed only 100 erasers, would your answer still be the same? Explain.

_____

_____

_____

_____

_____

Name _____

Write each number in standard form.

1. forty-three thousand, eight hundred five

   _____

2. 30 + 5,000 + 8 + 200 + 10,000

   _____

3. 90 hundreds + 7 tens + 100 ones

   _____

4. (6 × 100,000) + (2 × 1,000) + (5 × 10) + (4 × 1)

   _____

Solve. Show your mathematical thinking.

5. John is thinking of a number in the hundred thousands. The first digit is equal to the number of digits in the number. The number has twenty tens and twice as many thousands. The number of ones is an odd number that is less than 5 and greater than the digit in the hundreds place. What is John's number?

⚡ Reflect

If there are 20 tens in the number in problem 5, why is there a zero in the tens place?

_____

_____

_____

_____

_____

Name _____

Compare using **<**, **>**, or **=**.

1. 28,012 ◯ 20,812

2. 7 hundreds + 2 tens ◯ 60 tens + 20 ones

3. 1,868,213 ◯ 1,886,213

4. 30 thousands + 5 hundreds + 4 ones ◯ 3 ten thousands + 50 tens + 4 ones

Solve. Show your mathematical thinking.

5. Using the digits 4, 5, 3, 6, and 1, write three numbers—the smallest number possible, the largest number possible, and a number between the largest and smallest numbers.

Reflect

How many different numbers can be created that are in between the largest and smallest numbers in problem 5?

_____

_____

_____

_____

_____

_____

Name _____

Solve.

1. Round 389 to the nearest tens place. _____

2. Round 36,274 to the nearest thousands place. _____

3. Round 1,650,013 to the nearest hundred thousands place. _____

4. Round 2,047 to the nearest hundreds place. _____

Solve. Show your mathematical thinking.

5. Ticket sales for the 4 film festival days at the theater were 449, 512, 485, and 376. The theater had a goal of 2,000 tickets sold for the festival. Did they meet their goal? Why or why not?

☀ Reflect

If ticket sales for all 4 days had rounded to 500, would that definitely mean the goal was met? Explain.

_____

_____

_____

_____

_____

 © Carson-Dellosa · CD-104850 · Applying the Standards: Math

Name _____

Solve.

1.	4,891	2.	70,562	3.	5,636,541	4.	749,013
	− 2,178		+ 39,469		+ 274,932		− 56,048

Solve. Show your mathematical thinking.

5. Sarah added the numbers 325, 672, and 489 together. She said the total was 131,716. What did she do wrong?

☀ Reflect

How could Sarah have used estimation to know she had the incorrect answer?

_____

_____

_____

_____

_____

_____

Name _____

Solve.

1. 80
   × 5

2. 73
   × 6

3. 29
   × 8

4. 58
   × 4

Solve. Show your mathematical thinking.

5. How can addition help you solve 46 × 7? Write an equation to show your answer.

 **Reflect**

Explain another way to solve problem 5.

_____

_____

_____

_____

_____

Name _____

Solve.

1. 400
    × 9

2. 333
    × 7

3. 1,100
    × 3

4. 6,702
    × 8

Solve. Show your mathematical thinking.

5. Henry was creating a bar graph to show the results of his survey. He needed graph paper that would have a large enough area to show the data. Henry's survey had 3 possible choices and 125 survey participants. What is the least amount of square units the area of the graph paper must have to display the bar graph?

✺ **Reflect**

How would the area of the graph change if Henry wanted to add a square of space between each bar on the graph?

_____

_____

_____

_____

_____

Name _____

Solve.

1.   10
    × 40
    ‾‾‾‾

2.   30
    × 20
    ‾‾‾‾

3.   50
    × 50
    ‾‾‾‾

4.   80
    × 60
    ‾‾‾‾

Solve. Show your mathematical thinking.

5. Marisa wrote a rule for multiplying multiples of ten. She said that all products of multiples of ten will be a number in the thousands. Prove her rule true or false.

Reflect

Write your own rule for multiplying multiples of ten. Provide at least two examples.

_____

_____

_____

_____

_____

Name _____

Solve.

1. 17   2. 40   3. 65   4. 98
   × 15   × 23   × 74   × 56

Solve. Show your mathematical thinking.

5. The 6 key on Noah's calculator is broken. He needs to find the answer to 86 × 25. Show how Noah could use the distributive property and still use his calculator to solve the problem.

☀ Reflect

Explain how Noah could have used mental math to solve problem 5.

_____

_____

_____

_____

_____

Name _____

Solve.

1. $3\overline{)639}$ 2. $7\overline{)357}$ 3. $6\overline{)792}$ 4. $8\overline{)848}$

Solve. Show your mathematical thinking.

5. The dance team was arranging seats for its performance. They expected 225 people to attend, and they wanted to arrange the seats in fewer than 10 equal rows. How many rows and seats per row could they set up for the performance?

☀ Reflect

The dance team added 15 extra seats in an additional row in case more people came to the show. But, they still wanted an equal number of seats in each row. Explain a possible solution.

_____

_____

_____

_____

_____

© Carson-Dellosa · CD-104850 · Applying the Standards: Math

Name _____

Solve.

1. 7)‾4,900‾   2. 5)‾1,060‾   3. 4)‾9,572‾   4. 6)‾8,736‾

Solve. Show your mathematical thinking.

5. Jorge needs to eat 2,200 calories per day. He wants to divide the calories evenly between 4 small meals per day. How many calories will he need to eat per meal?

☀ Reflect

Explain how changing the number of meals a day would affect the calories Jorge should eat per meal?

_____

_____

_____

_____

_____

_____

_____

Name _____

Solve.

1. $4 \overline{)187}$ 2. $8 \overline{)846}$ 3. $5 \overline{)309}$ 4. $7 \overline{)251}$

Solve. Show your mathematical thinking.

5. Tyesha is reading a book with 292 pages. She has already read 69 of the pages. She typically reads 9 pages a night. How many more days will she need to read to finish the book?

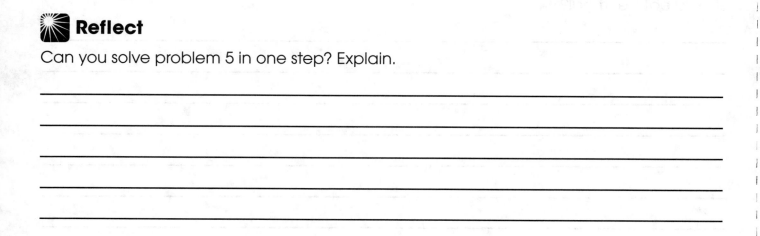

Reflect

Can you solve problem 5 in one step? Explain.

_____

_____

_____

_____

_____

          © Carson-Dellosa · CD-104850 · Applying the Standards: Math

Name _____

Solve.

1. $3\overline{)3,026}$ 2. $7\overline{)1,348}$ 3. $6\overline{)4,915}$ 4. $9\overline{)7,682}$

Solve. Show your mathematical thinking.

5. James solved the division problem below. What did he do wrong? How can he fix it?

$$
\begin{array}{r}
2,180 \ R2 \\
8\overline{)1,746} \\
\underline{16} \\
14 \\
\underline{8} \\
66 \\
\underline{64} \\
2
\end{array}
$$

 **Reflect**

Is it possible to divide the remainder equally by 8 also? Draw a picture to show your answer.

Name _____

Write the equivalent fractions.

1.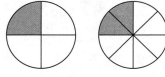

_____ = _____

2.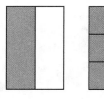

_____ = _____

3.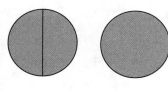

_____ = _____

4.

_____ = _____

Solve. Show your mathematical thinking.

5. Is it possible for a shape divided into thirds to show an equivalent fraction for $\frac{1}{2}$?

 **Reflect**

How could you make any fraction into one that is equivalent to $\frac{1}{2}$?

_____

_____

_____

_____

_____

Name _____

Complete the equivalent fractions.

1. $\dfrac{4}{5} = \dfrac{}{10}$

2. $\dfrac{2}{} = \dfrac{4}{6}$

3. $\dfrac{1}{4} = \dfrac{3}{}$

4. $\dfrac{}{8} = \dfrac{15}{24}$

Solve. Show your mathematical thinking.

5. Caleb said that $\dfrac{2}{4}$ is the same as $\dfrac{8}{16}$, but Melissa said it is the same as $\dfrac{1}{2}$. Who is correct? Why?

 **Reflect**

In what real-life situation might it be useful to change $\dfrac{1}{2}$ of something into $\dfrac{2}{4}$ or $\dfrac{8}{16}$?

_____

_____

_____

_____

_____

_____

Name _____

Write each fraction. Then, compare using **>**, **<**, or **=**.

1.

_____ ◯ _____

2.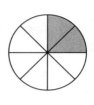

_____ ◯ _____

3.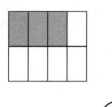

_____ ◯ _____

4.

_____ ◯ _____

Solve. Show your mathematical thinking.

5. Which hand has covered more distance from the 12 on a clock, the minute hand at 4:00 or the second hand at 15 seconds past? Write a fraction inequality to support your answer.

🌟 Reflect

What common denominator did you use for problem 5? Explain.

_____

_____

_____

_____

_____

Name _____

Compare using **>**, **<**, or **=**.

1. $\dfrac{5}{12}$ ◯ $\dfrac{3}{4}$ 2. $\dfrac{1}{4}$ ◯ $\dfrac{1}{6}$ 3. $\dfrac{7}{8}$ ◯ $\dfrac{28}{32}$ 4. $\dfrac{5}{10}$ ◯ $\dfrac{3}{6}$

Solve. Show your mathematical thinking.

5. Virginia has eaten 4 of the 6 slices of a pizza. Her mom tells her she has to give at least $\dfrac{1}{4}$ of the whole pizza to her brother. Does she have enough left to do that?

☀ Reflect

Is there pizza left over? What do you think the fair thing is for Virginia to do with it? Explain.

_____

_____

_____

_____

_____

Name _____

Solve.

1.  _____

2. ▯ + ▯ _____

3. $\frac{4}{10} + \frac{5}{10} =$ _____

4. $\frac{6}{9} + \frac{2}{9} =$ _____

Solve. Show your mathematical thinking.

5. Brian said that $\frac{1}{5} + \frac{1}{5}$ is $\frac{2}{10}$. Draw a picture to prove him right or wrong.

⁂ Reflect

Write a general rule for adding fractions.

_____

_____

_____

_____

Name _____

Solve.

1. $-$ = _____

2. $-$ = _____

3. $\dfrac{15}{20} - \dfrac{6}{20} =$ _____

4. $\dfrac{7}{8} - \dfrac{3}{8} =$ _____

Solve. Show your mathematical thinking.

5. Mrs. Santos had a dozen eggs. She has already used 3 of the eggs. What fraction of the original dozen does she have left?

✴ Reflect

Why might you not want to give the fractional answer to problem 5 in lowest terms? Explain.

_____

_____

_____

_____

Name _____

Write an addition equation that shows each fraction as a sum of three or more fractions.

1. $\dfrac{6}{6}$

_____

2. $\dfrac{5}{10}$

_____

3. $\dfrac{7}{8}$

_____

Solve. Show your mathematical thinking.

4. Brianna pulled an orange apart into 8 sections. What are 3 different ways she could share the orange between herself and her 2 friends? Write an equation using fractions to show each way.

![Reflect icon] **Reflect**

What fraction represents the whole orange in problem 4? How do you know?

_____

_____

_____

_____

_____

Name _____

Solve.

1. $3\frac{1}{3}$

   $+2\frac{1}{3}$
   _____

2. $1\frac{2}{9}$

   $+3\frac{4}{9}$
   _____

3. $5\frac{1}{5}$

   $+4\frac{3}{5}$
   _____

4. $3\frac{8}{12}$

   $+5\frac{5}{12}$
   _____

Solve. Show your mathematical thinking.

5. Jackie mixed $1\frac{3}{4}$ cups of whole wheat flour and $2\frac{1}{4}$ cups of all-purpose flour. Her recipe calls for 4 cups of flour. She thought she had $3\frac{4}{8}$ cups and would still need $\frac{4}{8}$ of a cup more. Does she need more or does she have enough? Explain and correct any mistakes Jackie may have made.

 **Reflect**

How could drawing a picture help you solve problem 5?

_____

_____

_____

_____

_____

Name _____

Solve.

1. $4\frac{2}{5}$
    $-3\frac{1}{5}$

2. $8\frac{4}{8}$
    $-2\frac{2}{8}$

3. $5\frac{6}{10}$
    $-1\frac{3}{10}$

4. $3\frac{3}{12}$
    $-2\frac{7}{12}$

Solve. Show your mathematical thinking.

5. A carpenter had a board that was $2\frac{5}{12}$ feet long. He cut off an 8-inch section. How long is the board now?

Reflect

Draw a picture of a yardstick to show the answer to problem 5.

Name _____

Solve.

1. Tony and Kristen ran a relay race together. Tony ran $\frac{3}{10}$ of a mile, and Kristen ran $\frac{5}{10}$ of a mile. How long was the race?

_____

2. Rain from a storm lasted for three days. Daily rainfall totals were $\frac{3}{8}$ inch, $3\frac{1}{8}$ inch, and $\frac{5}{8}$ inch. What was the total rainfall from the storm?

_____

Solve. Show your mathematical thinking.

3. The zoo committee voted to give the African animal zoologists $\frac{3}{12}$ of the land for elephants, $\frac{2}{12}$ of the land for lions, $\frac{1}{12}$ of the land for zebras, and another portion of the land for the smaller African animals. The Asian animal zoologists said this was not fair. Why?

 **Reflect**

If you were on the zoo committee, how would you make both the African and Asian animal zoologists happy?

_____

_____

_____

_____

_____

Name _____

Solve.

1. Mr. Taylor started his trip with $\frac{9}{10}$ of a tank of gas in the car. At the end of his trip, the car had $\frac{2}{10}$ of a tank left. How much gas did Mr. Taylor use on his trip?

_____

2. A deli customer bought $\frac{10}{16}$ of a pound of ham and $\frac{7}{16}$ of a pound of turkey. How much less turkey did she buy than ham?

_____

Solve. Show your mathematical thinking.

3. Benji estimates that he is $\frac{5}{8}$ of the way done making a model ship. If it has taken him 10 days to get this far, how many more days will it take for him to complete the model?

☀ Reflect

Why is it helpful to figure out how many days it took Benji to complete $\frac{1}{8}$ of the model?

_____

_____

_____

_____

    © Carson-Dellosa · CD-104850 · Applying the Standards: Math

Name _____

Write each fraction as the product of a whole number and a unit fraction.

1. _____

2. _____

3. _____

Solve. Show your mathmatical thinking.

4. Michael had a pool party. After the party, $\frac{5}{8}$ of a pepperoni pizza was left and $\frac{6}{8}$ of a cheese pizza was left. How many slices were left in all? Write two different fractions to show how much pizza was left.

 **Reflect**

Show how using a number line can help you solve problem 4.

Name _____

Solve. Write the answer in simplest form.

1. $5 \times \frac{3}{4} =$

2. $7 \times \frac{2}{9} =$

3. $\frac{5}{8} \times 4 =$

4. $\frac{1}{12} \times 8 =$

Solve. Show your mathematical thinking.

5. In Hector's closet, $\frac{3}{5}$ of the clothing have stripes, $\frac{2}{3}$ of the clothing is blue, and $\frac{1}{4}$ of the clothing are pants. None of the pants have stripes. If 60 pieces of clothing are in Hector's closet, what is the greatest number of pieces that could be a shirt without stripes?

 **Reflect**

How could drawing a model help you solve problem 5?

_____

_____

_____

_____

_____

  © Carson-Dellosa · CD-104850 · Applying the Standards: Math

Name _____

Solve. Write the answer in simplest form.

1. Each of Wendy's 3 cats eats $\frac{1}{4}$ cup of food in the morning. How much food does Wendy need in all for her cats each morning?

2. A hexagon measures $\frac{5}{8}$ inch per side. What is the hexagon's perimeter?

Solve. Show your mathematical thinking.

3. Ella read for $\frac{3}{4}$ of an hour every night for a week. Her weekly reading goal was 6 hours. Did she meet her goal?

✺ Reflect

How could you use quarters and dollars to help you solve problem 3?

_____

_____

_____

_____

Name _____

Solve.

1. If $\frac{4}{9}$ of the 27 students in the class are girls, how many students are boys?

2. The campers stopped to rest $\frac{3}{5}$ of the way into a 10-kilometer hike. How many kilometers had they already hiked?

Solve. Show your mathematical thinking.

3. Which fraction is greater, $\frac{2}{3}$ or $\frac{5}{8}$? _____

   Would you rather have $\frac{2}{3}$ of a 9-inch candy bar or $\frac{5}{8}$ of a 10-inch candy bar? Why?

 **Reflect**

Is $\frac{1}{2}$ of one whole always the same amount as $\frac{1}{2}$ of a different whole? Explain.

_____

_____

_____

_____

 © Carson-Dellosa · CD-104850 · Applying the Standards: Math

Name _____

Solve.

1. $\dfrac{5}{10} = \dfrac{}{100}$

2. $\dfrac{80}{100} = \dfrac{}{10}$

3. $\begin{array}{r} \dfrac{4}{10} \\[4pt] \dfrac{3}{100} \\[2pt] +\phantom{\dfrac{3}{100}} \end{array}$

4. $\begin{array}{r} \dfrac{78}{100} \\[4pt] \dfrac{2}{10} \\[2pt] +\phantom{\dfrac{2}{10}} \end{array}$

Solve. Show your mathematical thinking.

5. Hannah had 5 dimes and 22 pennies. What fraction of a dollar did she have?

 **Reflect**

How many $\dfrac{1}{10}$ are in $\dfrac{1}{100}$? How do you know?

_____

_____

_____

_____

_____

Name _____

Write each fraction as a decimal.

1. $\frac{3}{10}$ = _____

2. $\frac{50}{100}$ = _____

3. $\frac{87}{100}$ = _____

4. $\frac{9}{100}$ = _____

Solve. Show your mathematical thinking.

5. Timothy has a jar of 648 pennies. What fraction of dollars does he have? How should he record the total with a dollar sign and decimal point?

 **Reflect**

Why do you think decimal notation is used for money instead of mixed numbers? Are there any places where you might see mixed numbers or fractions for cents used regularly for money? Explain.

_____

_____

_____

_____

_____

Name _____

Compare using >, <, or =.

1. 0.6 ◯ 0.9   2. 0.72 ◯ 0.27   3. 0.05 ◯ 0.50   4. 0.8 ◯ 0.80

Solve. Show your mathematical thinking.

5. Becky's teacher gave her the 7 tiles below. She was instructed to sort the tiles into three piles: closest to 0, closest to 0.5, and closest to 1. Sort the tiles for Becky and then create and sort additional tiles to have an equal number of tiles in each pile.

| 1.05 | 0.43 | 0.76 | 0.21 | 0.09 | 0.9 | 0.67 |

Reflect

What would be the greatest digit in the tenths place of the decimals in the "closest to 0" pile? Hundredths place? Explain.

_____

_____

_____

_____

_____

_____

Name _____

Write the equivalent measurement.

1. 4 kg = _____ g

2. 6 ft. = _____ in.

3. 28 m = _____ cm

4. _____ oz. = 9 lb.

Solve. Show your mathematical thinking.

5. Jason found part of a conversion table in the back of his math book. The table had some missing numbers and was not labeled with units of measurement. Help Jason figure out what units are being converted and complete the chart.

	1				5
		120			300

Reflect

What other unit conversion could the chart be describing? Explain.

_____

_____

_____

_____

_____

Name _____

Solve.

1. Five members of the track team ran a relay race in which each leg of the race was 400 meters. How many kilometers long was the entire race?

_____

2. Javon was filling a tub with water to bathe his dog. The tub could hold 20 gallons. Javon had only a quart pitcher to use to fill the tub. How many times would he need to fill the pitcher to fill the tub?

_____

3. A baker used 1 kilogram of flour and 200 grams of sugar in a recipe. Which ingredient did he use more of? How much more?

_____

Solve. Show your mathematical thinking.

4. Four children in a family each drink 200 milliliters of juice per meal. If they eat 3 meals a day, how many liters of juice will the family need to buy for the week?

☀ Reflect

Will the family have juice leftover at the end of the week? Explain.

_____

_____

_____

_____

Name _____

Solve.

1. David read for 25 minutes each day for a week. For how many hours and minutes did he read?

_____

2. Sierra left school at 3:40 pm. She stopped next door at the library for 25 minutes, and it took 15 minutes to bike home. What time did she arrive home?

_____

Solve. Show your mathematical thinking.

3. Oliver's smartphone recorded that he woke up 3 times an hour for 2 minutes each time. If he went to bed at 10:00 pm and woke up at 6:00 am, how many seconds of sleep did he lose?

☀ Reflect

Do you divide or multiply to go from a larger unit of measure to a smaller unit of measure? Explain.

_____

_____

_____

_____

_____

Name _____

Solve.

1. India bought a welcome-to-school pencil for each of the 134 new fourth-graders. Each pencil cost 8¢. How much money did she spend?

_____

2. Evan paid for his $8.75 movie ticket with a twenty-dollar bill. What bills and coins will he get in change?

_____

Solve. Show your mathematical thinking.

3. Peter saved 2 twenty-dollar bills, 3 ten-dollar bills, 1 five-dollar bill, and 12 one-dollar bills. His little brother Sean saved 2 twenty-dollar bills, 1 ten-dollar bill, 23 one-dollar bills, and 30 quarters. Which brother saved more money? How much more?

☀ Reflect

How could you use a table to help you quickly add the totals in problem 3?

_____

_____

_____

_____

_____

Name _____

Find the perimeter.

1. 9 in. /\ 6 in.
    /‾‾‾‾\
    13 in.

    _____

2. 79 km
    ▱
    48 km

    _____

3. 117 ft.
    90 ft. /‾‾‾‾\ 81 ft.
    152 ft.

    _____

Solve. Show your mathematical thinking.

4. Andrew is making a picture frame for his favorite poster. He has one piece of edging that is 20 feet long. His poster is 40 inches by 28 inches. If he wants to make a second poster frame with the leftover edging, what is the largest frame he can make?

☀ Reflect

If Andrew's 20 feet of edging came in two 10-foot sections instead of one piece, how would that affect your answer?

_____

_____

_____

_____

_____

Name _____

Find the area.

1.
15 cm

_____

2.
27 mm
12 mm

_____

3.
9 ft.
6 ft.

_____

Solve. Show your mathematical thinking.

4. Ansley's backyard will be divided into two sections—a grass area and a patio. If the backyard measures 32 yards by 27 yards, and she wants at least $\frac{2}{3}$ of her backyard to be grass, what dimensions could her patio be?

⚡ Reflect

How could you use a trick for finding multiples of 9 to solve problem 4?

_____

_____

_____

_____

_____

Name _____

Find the area and perimeter.

1. A square has a perimeter of 28 inches. What is its area?

   _____

2. A rectangular playground has an area of 414 square meters and a perimeter of 72 meters. What are its dimensions?

   _____

Solve. Show your mathematical thinking.

3. Mrs. Suarez wants a garden with an area of 96 square yards and wants to spend the least amount possible on fencing. What dimensions should her garden be?

☀ Reflect

What is the greatest perimeter possible for problem 3? Would that garden be practical? Explain.

_____

_____

_____

_____

_____

Name _____

Use the line plot to answer the questions.

1. How many plants were measured?

   _____

2. What is the difference in growth
   between the plant that grew the
   most and the plant that grew the least?

   _____

3. What fraction of the plants showed at
   least $\frac{1}{2}$ inch of growth?

   _____

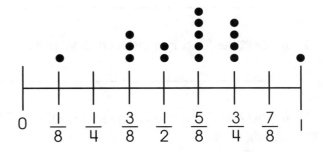

Plant Growth in Inches

Solve. Show your mathematical thinking.

4. Maria said that the greatest number of plants grew 1 inch in a month. Sabena said
   Maria read the line plot incorrectly. Explain Maria's mistake. What number of plants
   actually grew 1 inch? How many inches did the greatest number of plants grow?

✺ Reflect

Assuming the plants were all the same type, were planted at the same time, and got
the same care, how could you explain any outliers in the data? *Outliers* are data points
that stand out, such as any plants that grew a lot more or a lot less than the average.

_____

_____

_____

_____

_____

Name _____

Solve.

1. If you are facing east and you turn 90° to your right, in what direction are you now facing?

   _____

2. If you are facing north and you turn to face south, how many degrees did you turn?

   _____

3. If you are facing north and make a 360° turn, in which direction are you now facing?

   _____

Solve. Show your mathematical thinking.

4. If you were facing north and turned 90° to the right three times, what direction would you be facing? How many 90° turns to the right will it take to put you facing in the same direction in which you began?

Reflect

How does knowing how many 90° turns are in a full circle help you answer problem 4?

_____

_____

_____

_____

_____

Name _____

Solve.

1. How many degrees does the minute hand on a clock move each minute?

_____

2. How many degrees does the hour hand move each hour?

_____

3. What time is it if the hour hand is between the 2 and the 3 and the minute hand moved 120° past the 12?

_____

Solve. Show your mathematical thinking.

4. What angle is made by the hour and minute hand at 3:30? How many degrees has the minute hand moved since 3:00?

Reflect

What angle do the quarter hours on a clock correspond to?

_____

_____

_____

_____

_____

Name _____

Measure each angle with a protractor.

1.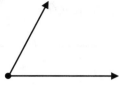

_____

2.

_____

3.

_____

Solve. Show your mathematical thinking.

4. Warren cut 2 pizzas in different ways. Which pizza's slices form greater angles? If he ate 2 pieces of one pizza and 3 pieces of the other pizza as shown, about what fraction of a full pizza did he eat? Use angle measures to justify your answer.

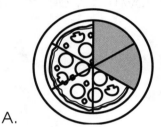

A.

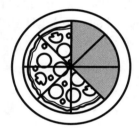

B.

⁂ Reflect

How could you have used division instead of a protractor to find the angle of each pizza slice tip?

_____

_____

_____

_____

_____

Name _____

Draw an angle to match each given measure.

1. 110°   2. 35°   3. 142°

Solve. Show your mathematical thinking.

4. A sundial is a tool that tells the time based on the angle of the shadow cast by the sun. Reese uses the sundial at the park to know when it is time to go home in time for dinner each day. Reese arrives when the shadow is at an 86° angle and leaves when it is at a 168° angle. If noon is a 90° angle, how long does Reese spend at the park each day?

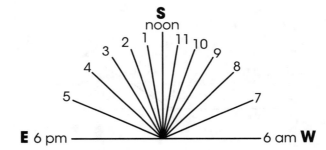

![Reflect] **Reflect**

Why do you think the hours on the sundial are not evenly spaced? How might this affect your answer?

_____

_____

_____

_____

_____

Name _____

Write an equation to solve for the unknown angle.

1.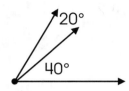

_____

2.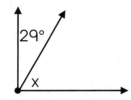

_____

3.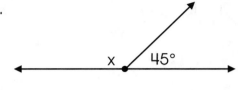

_____

Solve. Show your mathematical thinking.

4. Two angles with a sum of 180° are *supplementary angles*. Two angles with a sum of 90° are *complementary angles*. Find the values of x and y in the diagram below if 55° + x = 90°. Which other pairs of angles are complementary?

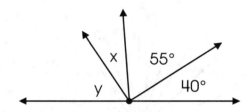

Reflect

Shade the complementary angles in the diagram above with red and the supplementary angles with green. Write equations for each pair below to prove that they are complementary or supplementary.

_____

_____

_____

_____

Name _____

Use the points to name each line, line segment, or ray.

1.

_____

2.

_____

3.

_____

4.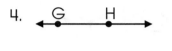

_____

Solve. Show your mathematical thinking.

5. Draw a map of a neighborhood. The main business street is $\overleftrightarrow{AC}$ Avenue. The main residential street, $\overrightarrow{BD}$ Street, starts at $\overrightarrow{AC}$ Avenue. A short dead-end street is on either side of $\overrightarrow{BD}$ Street, $\overline{DE}$ Road and $\overline{DF}$ Lane.

✹ Reflect

Should $\overrightarrow{BD}$ Street be a one-way street? Explain.

_____

_____

_____

_____

_____

Name _____

Name each angle and label as *right, acute,* or *obtuse.*

1.

_____

2.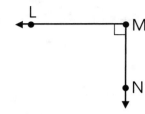

_____

3.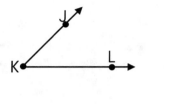

_____

4.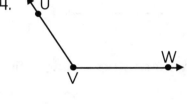

_____

Solve. Show your mathematical thinking.

5. Draw a quadrilateral with at least 1 of each type of angle, right, acute, and obtuse. Is it possible to draw a triangle with 1 of each angle type? Is it possible to draw a quadrilateral with all acute angles? Explain.

 **Reflect**

As you were solving problem 5, what did you notice about the total degrees the angles of a triangle add up to?

_____

_____

_____

_____

Name _____

Label each figure as *perpendicular, parallel,* or *intersecting.*

1.

_____

2.

_____

3.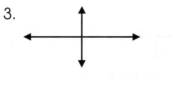

_____

4.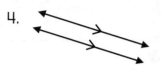

_____

Solve. Show your mathematical thinking.

5. Name the line segments in the graph with ordered pairs for their end points.

_____

Which line segments are parallel? _____

Are any line segments perpendicular? _____

How could you change the point at (5, 1) to make the segment between 4 and 5 perpendicular to the segment between 3 and 4?

_____

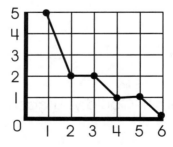

 **Reflect**

How could the grid behind the graph help you answer the questions in problem 5?

_____

_____

Name _____

Name each polygon.

1. This figure has 4 right angles and 2 pairs of parallel line segments that are all congruent.

   _____

2. This figure has 4 sets of congruent parallel line segments, but no perpendicular line segments. All of its angles are obtuse.

   _____

3. This figure has 2 parallel line segments, 2 acute angles, and 2 obtuse angles.

   _____

Solve. Show your mathematical thinking.

4. Write directions for drawing a cube by describing its edges, its angles, and how the faces are positioned in relationship to each other, using the words *parallel* and *perpendicular.*

 **Reflect**

Follow your directions from problem 4. Could you accurately form a cube from your directions?

Name _____

Identify each triangle as *right, obtuse,* or *acute.* Then, identify each triangle as *scalene, isosceles,* or *equilateral.*

1.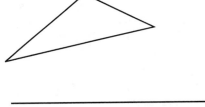

    _____

    _____

2.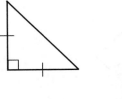

    _____

    _____

3.

    _____

    _____

4.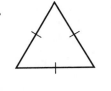

    _____

    _____

Solve. Show your mathematical thinking.

5. Draw an equilateral triangle. Draw three lines inside the triangle to form 6 right triangles.

🔆 **Reflect**

What is the sum of the angles that share the same vertex from the 6 triangles in problem 5?

_____

_____

_____

_____

Name _____

Draw the line or lines of symmetry for each figure. If the figure does not have a line of symmetry, circle it.

1.
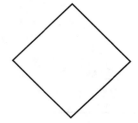

2.
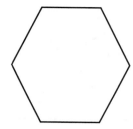

3.
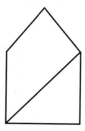

4.
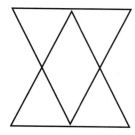

Solve. Show your mathematical thinking.

5. The city has a rectangular field with a perimeter of 80 meters and an area of 300 square meters. City officials would like to divide the field symmetrically to create a dog park and a playground. How should the field be divided to give the best arrangement and space for the dog park and the playground?

 **Reflect**

If the city officials decide to divide the field for a batting cage and an outdoor bowling lane, would this change your answer? Explain.

_____

_____

_____

Answer Key

Answers to some higher-level problems will vary but may include the answers provided. For all Reflect responses, accept all reasonable answers as long as students have proper evidence and support.

Page 5

1. 3 × 6 = 18; 2. 8 × 2 = 16;
3. 4 × 9 = 36; 4. 3 years

Page 6

1. 42 toy robots; 2. $8; 3. maple; The maple tree increased by 7 times, while the oak tree only increased by 6 times.

Page 7

1. 5 erasers; 2. 18 goals; 3. 39 8-person tables and 3 6-person tables

Page 8

1. 1, 18; 2, 9; 3, 6; 2. 1, 55; 5, 11;
3. 1, 36; 2, 18; 3, 12; 4, 9; 6, 6; 4. 1, 63;
3, 21; 7, 9; 5. 5 feet × 6 feet

Page 9

1. 8, 12, 16, 20, 24, 28, 32, 36, 40, 44, 48, 52, 56, 60, 64, 68, 72, 76, 80, 84, 88, 92, 96, 100; 2. 5, 10, 15, 20, 25, 30, 35, 40, 45, 50, 55, 60, 65, 70, 75, 80, 85, 90, 95, 100; 3. 11, 22, 33, 44, 55, 66, 77, 88, 99; 4. 9, 18, 27, 36, 45, 54, 63, 72, 81, 90, 99; 5. 9 groups of 3 and 9 groups of 6

Page 10

1. composite; 2. prime; 3. composite; 4. prime; 5. 2 is an even number and a prime number; 15 is an odd number and a composite number

Page 11

1. 24, 29, 34; 2. 768; 3,072; 12,288;
3. 26, 23, 30; 4. 78, 80, 240; 5. 19 miles

Page 12

1. ☐; 2. [grid image]; 3. ☒; 4. 24 dark stones (length of light stone square × 4 + 4)

Page 13

1. 40; 2. 70; 3. 2; 4. 500; 5. bulk store for $50/1,000

Page 14

1. 43,805; 2. 15,238; 3. 9,170;
4. 602,054; 5. 640,203

Page 15

1. >; 2. >; 3. <; 4. =; 5. 13,456; 65,431; 43,615

Page 16

1. 390; 2. 36,000; 3. 1,700,000;
4. 2,000; 5. no; 400 + 500 + 500 + 400 = 1,800

Page 17

1. 2,713; 2. 110,031; 3. 5,911,473;
4. 692,965; 5. 1,486; She did not carry the tens and hundreds. She just wrote them beside the ones and tens in the answer.

Page 18

1. 400; 2. 438; 3. 232; 4. 232; 5. (40 × 7) + (6 × 7) = 280 + 42 = 322

Page 19

1. 3,600; 2. 2,331; 3. 3,300; 4. 53,616;
5. 375 sq. units

Page 20

1. 400; 2. 600; 3. 2,500; 4. 4,800;
5. false; 10 × 10 = 100

Page 21

1. 255; 2. 920; 3. 4,810; 4. 5,488; 5. (80 × 25) + (5 × 25) + 25 = 2,150

Page 22

1. 213; 2. 51; 3. 132; 4. 106; 5. 9 rows of 25 or 5 rows of 45

Page 23

1. 700; 2. 212; 3. 2,393; 4. 1,456; 5. 550 calories per meal

Page 24

1. 46 r3; 2. 105 r6; 3. 61 r4; 4. 35 r6;
5. 25 days

Page 25

1. 1,008 r2; 2. 192 r4; 3. 819 r1; 4. 853 r5;
5. James started putting the answer over the 1 instead of over the 7 (8 goes into 17 two times, not into 1 two times).

Page 26

1. $\frac{1}{4} = \frac{2}{8}$; 2. $\frac{1}{2} = \frac{3}{6}$; 3. $\frac{2}{2} = 1$; 4. $\frac{3}{4} = \frac{6}{8}$;
5. The circle could be divided into sixths. $\frac{3}{6} = \frac{1}{2}$

Page 27

1. $\frac{8}{10}$; 2. $\frac{2}{3}$; 3. $\frac{3}{12}$; 4. $\frac{5}{8}$; 5. They are both correct.

Page 28

1. $\frac{3}{4} > \frac{2}{4}$; 2. $\frac{1}{4} = \frac{2}{8}$; 3. $\frac{3}{8} < \frac{1}{2}$; 4. $\frac{1}{3} > \frac{2}{8}$;
5. $\frac{4}{12} > \frac{15}{60}$

Page 29

1. <; 2. >; 3. =; 4. =; 5. yes; $\frac{1}{3} > \frac{1}{4}$

Page 30

1. $\frac{3}{4}$; 2. $\frac{2}{3}$; 3. $\frac{9}{10}$; 4. $\frac{8}{9}$; 5. $\frac{2}{5}$;
Brian mistakenly added the denominators.

Page 31

1. $\frac{3}{4} - \frac{2}{4} = \frac{1}{4}$; 2. $\frac{4}{6} - \frac{3}{6} = \frac{1}{6}$; 3. $\frac{9}{20}$;
4. $\frac{4}{8}$ or $\frac{1}{2}$; 5. $\frac{9}{12}$ or $\frac{3}{4}$

Page 32

1. $\frac{1}{6} + \frac{1}{6} + \frac{1}{6} + \frac{3}{6}$; 2. $\frac{1}{10} + \frac{1}{10} + \frac{3}{10}$; 3. $\frac{2}{8} + \frac{2}{8} + \frac{2}{8} + \frac{1}{8}$; 4. $\frac{2}{8} + \frac{2}{8} + \frac{4}{8}$; $\frac{3}{8} + \frac{3}{8} + \frac{2}{8}$; $\frac{1}{8} + \frac{3}{8} + \frac{4}{8}$

Page 33

1. $5\frac{2}{3}$; 2. $4\frac{6}{9}$ or $4\frac{2}{3}$; 3. $9\frac{4}{5}$; 4. $9\frac{1}{12}$;
5. She has 4 cups; Her mistake was adding the denominators so she did not recognize that the fractions make another whole cup.

Page 34

1. $1\frac{1}{5}$; 2. $6\frac{2}{8}$ or $6\frac{1}{4}$; 3. $4\frac{3}{10}$; 4. $\frac{8}{12}$ or $\frac{2}{3}$;
5. $1\frac{9}{12}$ or $1\frac{3}{4}$ feet

Page 35

1. $\frac{8}{10}$ or $\frac{4}{5}$ of a mile; 2. $4\frac{1}{8}$ inches;
3. The African animals got more than $\frac{1}{2}$ of the available land.

Page 36

1. $\frac{7}{10}$ tank; 2. $2\frac{3}{16}$ pound; 3. 6 days

Answer Key

Page 37

1. $3 \times \frac{1}{4}$; 2. $5 \times \frac{1}{6}$; 3. $2 \times \frac{1}{3}$; 4. 11 slices; $\frac{11}{8}$ or $1\frac{3}{8}$

Page 38

1. $3\frac{3}{4}$; 2. $1\frac{5}{9}$; 3. $2\frac{1}{2}$; 4. $\frac{2}{3}$; 5. 9 pieces

Page 39

1. $\frac{3}{4}$ cup; 2. $3\frac{3}{4}$ inches; 3. no; $5\frac{1}{4}$ hours

Page 40

1. $\frac{5}{9}$; 2. 6 km; 3. $\frac{2}{3}$; $\frac{5}{8}$ of 10 is greater than 6 inches, which is $\frac{2}{3}$ of 9.

Page 41

1. $\frac{50}{100}$; 2. $\frac{8}{10}$; 3. $\frac{43}{100}$; 4. $\frac{98}{100}$; 5. $\frac{72}{100}$

Page 42

1. 0.3; 2. 0.50; 3. 0.87; 4. 0.09; 5. $6\frac{48}{100}$; $6.48

Page 43

1. <; 2. >; 3. <; 4. =; 5. closest to 0: 0.09, 0.21; closest to 0.5: 0.43, 0.67; closest to 1: 0.76, 0.9, 1.05; One additional tile should be added to *closest to 0* and *closest to 0.5*. Answers will vary.

Page 44

1. 4,000 g; 2. 72 in.; 3. 2,800 cm; 4. 144 oz.; 5. could be minutes and seconds or hours and minutes;

min.	1	2	3	4	5
sec.	60	120	180	240	300

Page 45

1. 2 km; 2. 80 times; 3. flour; 800 g; 4. 17 L

Page 46

1. 2 hr. 55 min; 2. 4:20; 3. 2,880 sec.

Page 47

1. $10.72; 2. 1 ten, 1 one, 1 quarter; 3. Peter; $6.50

Page 48

1. 28 in.; 2. 254 km; 3. 440; 4. 26 in. × 26 in.

Page 49

1. 225 sq. cm; 2. 324 sq. mm; 3. 117 sq. ft.; 4. 18 yd. × 16 yd. or 32 yd. × 9 yd.

Page 50

1. 49 sq. in.; 2. 23 m × 18 m; 3. 8 yd. × 12 yd.

Page 51

1. 16 plants; 2. $\frac{7}{8}$ in.; 3. $\frac{12}{16}$ or $\frac{3}{4}$; 4. Maria thought the greatest value along the number line was the greatest number of plants. The most plants grew $\frac{5}{8}$ in. where 5 dots are shown above that value.

Page 52

1. south; 2. 180°; 3. north; 4. west, 1

Page 53

1. 6°; 2. 30°; 3. 2:20; 4. 90° or 75° to account for the hour hand being halfway between the 3 and 4 at 3:30. 180°

Page 54

1. 62°; 2. 153°; 3. 14°; 4. A (60°) > B (45°)

Page 55

1. ____; 2. ____; 3. ____; 4. about 6 hours each day

Page 56

1. 20° + 40° = 60°; 2. 90° = 29° + 61°; 3. 180° – 45° = 135°; 4. x = 35°, y = 50°; y and 40° are complementary

Page 57

1. *EF*; 2. *NO*; 3. *HI*; 4. *GH*;

5.

Page 58

1. *STU*, obtuse; 2. *LMN*, right; 3. *JKL*, acute; 4. *UVW*, obtuse; 5. no, no; Check students' reasoning.

Page 59

1. intersecting lines; 2. parallel lines; 3. perpendicular intersecting lines; 4. parallel lines; 5. (1, 5)(2, 2); (2, 2) (3, 2); (3, 2)(4, 1); (4, 1)(5, 1); (5, 1)(6, 0); parallel: (2, 2)(3, 2) with (4, 1)(5, 1) and (3, 2)(4, 1) with (5, 1)(6, 0); none are perpendicular; (5, 2)

Page 60

1. square; 2. octagon; 3. trapezoid; 4. Answers will vary.

Page 61

1. obtuse, scalene; 2. right, isosceles; 3. right, scalene; 4. acute, equilateral; 5. Check students' drawings.

Page 62

1. ⊠ 2. ⬡ 3. ◯ 4. ⊞;
5. Answers will vary.